Gallery Books
Editor Peter Fallon
INFINITY POOL

Vona Groarke

INFINITY POOL

Gallery Books

Infinity Pool
is first published
simultaneously in paperback
and in a clothbound edition
on 22 May 2025.

The Gallery Press
Loughcrew
Oldcastle
County Meath
Ireland

www.gallerypress.com

*All rights reserved. For permission
to reprint or broadcast these poems,
write to The Gallery Press:*
books@gallerypress.com

© Vona Groarke 2025

The right of Vona Groarke to be identified as Author of this
Work has been asserted in accordance with Section 77 of the
Copyright, Designs and Patents Act 1988.

ISBN 978 1 91737 108 7 *paperback*
      978 1 91737 109 4 *clothbound*

A CIP catalogue record for this book
is available from the British Library.

Infinity Pool receives financial assistance
from the Arts Council of Ireland.

Contents

Stansted to Knock, December 21st *page* 9
With the moon in full spate such that 10
Infinity Pool 11
An Poll Gorm / The Blue Hole 12
Inner Space 13
Nocturne With Ink 14
Imagine the Atlantic as an Actor 16
Imagine the Atlantic as a Mechanic 17
The Tell 18
Mise en Scène 20
Lint 22
Setting My Mother's Hair as an *Ars Poetica* 24
Imagine the Atlantic as a Journalist 25
Imagine the Atlantic as a Chambermaid 26
The Low Road 27
Proposition 28
Still Life in Marble 29
Tipping Point 33
What the day offers, so the day demands 34
May the Tenth 36
Snapshot 37
Two Kinds of Ending 38
Imagine the Atlantic as a Film-maker 39
Imagine the Atlantic as a Bartender 40
The Future of the Poem 41
In the Cemetery of Non-existent Cemeteries, Gdańsk 44
Hindsight 45
Short Poem About Self-consciousness 46
Introduction 47
Imagine the Atlantic as an Artist 48
Imagine the Atlantic as a Poet 49
The Copybook 50
Ending Without a Poem 51
My Own Fourth Wall 52
Reading Chinese Love Poems in a Borrowed English House 54

Acknowledgements 63

Stansted to Knock, December 21st

Floored by clouds so dense you think you
could hopscotch over them, no problem,
or loll there, palmed and cushioned
in a sunlit evermore, we are barely
a couple of toy, plexiglass panes
away from our own private sun.

Here I am open, riddled with light,
my full year split like a pomegranate,
all its days beaded like seeds,
no, not seeds, like quartz
on a passage tomb the rising sun
had flicked to light this morning,

a light I myself am so in need of,
for my soul (for lack of a better word)
in its tiny, gilded cage that I buff up
maybe once a year (and this is that once),
to rejoin the rest of me, as a plane
touches down on its shadow, minutely.

What seemed impossible up there,
namely hurt, namely flaw,
clumps to a mizzling afternoon
as we begin descent. Clouds crowd us,
muffle, buffet, quell, but we're close now,
only minutes away from stepping out

into lives we chose, even bought tickets to,
where a future, like luggage carouseled
before we're through passport control,
will be waiting for us to say it is ours,
to be surprised to find it so heavy,
dumbfounded to find it so light.

With the moon in full spate such that

you could read by it if you took
your book and your eyes outside
and opened them both to the cold
questions asked by rooftiles and
windows and gateposts and roads
on a night when even trees
are all agape

and your own mouth's full
of small, round words like pebbles
or glass beads smoothed by usage,
silvered by hand or, in much the same vein,
by a moon described as being in full spate

such that they answer
each by each when called upon
and most correctly:
I do now.

Infinity Pool

I had it in the night, the image,
but lacked the energy or will
to magic my body through
my own fourth wall and lower
myself, spit-spot, into the page.

I saw, I just about recall,
a blue rectangle not quite blank
held up against blue sky, blue sea,
so you weren't supposed to tell
the edge, the stitching or the seams.

And I am folding it now, this pool,
corner to corner, line to line,
so as to carry about with me
its deep blue scrap of lie.

But carrying folded water
isn't feasible. You know that.

An Poll Gorm / *The Blue Hole*

The Atlantic agrees the cement wall
only if, twice a day, by appointment,
it gets to roughhouse and tousle it,
pretending to hold it under and then,
all kindness, just at the last minute,
letting it up to grab at air, then lull.

Which is where I come in, over the rocks,
bringing my one and only body to a pool
barely brimming the visible wall
that promises to play nice with me,
all the sea's knots unknotted,
all its quarrels quelled.

First the squall of skin and sea then,
gently, I quiet to its quiet, begin
to feel as though my life thus far,
every second of it, is what's under me,
keeping me up, and my future, a life-mask
of sky fitted, weightless, to my face.

I stay in until the water tires of me, climb
out into a day along the spine of which
I'll find myself licking salt from my forearm
so that my tongue is stars in darkness,
my mind a fossil in gaunt sun, losing
less than I thought, growing old.

Inner Space

n. — the environment beneath the surface of the sea

A chance remark, something of nothing,
a car slowing on the road at my door,
the way you think it's in the past and then
and then away I go on a cormorant dive
down through the foam of an afternoon,
through whatever current slaps dabberlock,
bladderwrack or a mermaid's purse of words,
unwords and stingy silence any-which-way
against my foolish skin. Down past questions
with flotsam answers I can't quite get a hand
to. Down past wave upon wave of longing,
through the deeps of what there's no time for,
past sunlight suturing its own every last gape.
Down through the roar an ocean clenches tight
as a stiletto. Down to a blackness so entire
I think I'm standing, eyes closed, in the yard
in August, held tilted back to the Pleiades
so every firing Yes drops in my mouth
and I rise to it, cormorant hell-bent on sky
with a little fish tucked by me in its beak.

Nocturne With Ink

I expect it any minute to sneak free
of clouds and trees and roofs
and to shimmy into its rightful slot
in the corner of a skylight with my desk
one side and the world the other,
the world with you in it.

How can it be
that I think of you now
as someone from the past?

When it lands it turns out
to be scratchy moonlight
like ten-day-old stubble
on the face of a world
I hear scuffling and finicking
out there all day, talking to itself.

Still. It's something, the light.
And you, presumably, breathe
a version of it deep in your lungs
and out again into air I breathe
deep in my lungs and out again
so we're not entirely lost to one another,
not in the firmament, where it matters,
though I'm sure you don't think so.

Nor do I, not really,
with all this elsewise
passing through my days:
moonlight through skylight,
words through ink, time
through body, love through
whatever love passes through
working its way free.

You'll be sleeping now, your mind
unriddled and far away
from this time-lag cottage

where I live in writing
moonlight on two
sides of the
one page.

Imagine the Atlantic as an Actor

running lines. He tries out emphasis
as if dropping stones in a rockpool
(I sink. *I* sink. I *sink*.), and plays along
with a smoky grin or countermanding fist.

Imagine him walking his soliloquy
over the bar of the man-made pool
past cue card, prompter or spike marks
and off, quite simply, off into the wings.

Just ripples of applause, he thinks,
nothing to rise from pit or stalls
to come at him awash in footlights,
bearing down on his exit line.

Tomorrow, he thinks, for the matinee,
he will say the odd word twice,
see if anyone shifts in their velvet seats,
if anybody past the shoreline blinks.

Imagine the Atlantic as a Mechanic

who knows full well where every tool and implement should be,
on its nail on the panel above the workbench, inside a dark outline
of itself that somebody painted nice and neat at the very start of this

just as each wreck on the ocean floor sits intact in its mould of water
and every boat drags with it an anchor of shadow, and every vessel,
including the body, slits into the surface a shape it already makes.

Wouldn't you like to live this way too, every move foreshadowed
by a course determined way back and designed especially for you?
All your necessaries to hand, first the outline, then the infill; first,

the need and then the need rounded off and satisfied. You don't even
have to look, that's how well this works. Need a pliers? You reach out
and the pliers is right there. Need a future? There it is, in a deep, dark line

drawn by someone, you don't know who or remember standing oh so still
for the paintbrush to follow your cast and gist, and never touch but chase
the edge of you to show where you're not or where you used to be.

The Tell

If I say it was something I honed,
nursed, spooned, told stories to,
brushed its yellow hair
and shined its shoes

will you know what it is
I write about?

What if I tell you
now and then
we'd undertake
a day trip to the sea
where I'd train it
to smile at other smiles,
say only so many words
and nothing more?

It was a quick learner, give it that.

I showed it a shed where I'd coupled, once,
and we looked in restaurant windows
where people never turned our way
for all their fiddling with cutlery,
looking as if they held nothing back.

We sat on a wall and ate ice-cream cones,
watched a white coffin tunnelling through
two lines of grey school uniforms
into the maw of a grey church.

Which fairly put a stop
to our shenanigans.

Closer yet? (Yours, I can agree,
is the hard part.)

Therefore, a clue: at night, since then
we sometimes carry one chair each
out in the yard to watch the house,
one room alight with our not being there.

Mise en Scène

when summer's a word typed in black ink
and the peony has rusted in the rain

when you're wearing lambswool in July
and sweeping fallen leaves
from the kitchen floor

when you pick up Friday
where you put down Thursday
and think it hardly matters
either way

when the man who calls to the door
calls you by someone else's name

when the radio flinches
from its lead-lined news

when that scrappy cat
with the bile-yellow eyes
won't budge for shoo nor clap
from your window

when an airlift helicopter spidering
from one edge of the skylight
to the other is bad news
(not yours, for now)

when you dream of water
and can't figure out what dreaming
of water is meant to signify

when you feel far removed from
an ocean that's only a mountain
and a bare half hour away

that's even now sawing itself in half
then sewing itself together
one more time

well there you are

solved by water
redressed

so the night sits
backdropped

hoped for

right in itself

Lint

See, here's the thing:
I'm grating lemons on a mandoline
that was my mother's mandoline
well before it was mine

and that's how the thought
doubles back on itself
like a hand that
after the zesting is done
still holds the shape of the lemon
in its knuckles, in its grip

that back when my mother
was grating lemons on this mandoline
I too was grabbing at ways
a young woman back there back then
could make something of herself.

Paperbacks, music, hair dye, boots —
I went at it with everything I had;
year on year, plan after plan,
everything pressed
to the purposeful surface
of my desiring.

Come the day I began to feel
like a moth on the wrong side
of a darkening window.

Then the voices turned off, like a radio,
and coats on the coat stand
grew dust in the hall.

And so, when I wasn't so young,
I slept in a bed with a cover of figs

and spilling pomegranates,
so my body could be wishful too

while I was dreaming of so much to come
I could make a tight, crammed ball of it,
like lint, and still it would spring out,
in a heartbeat, to a sky.

Where did it go, all that future:
did I pass through it like a car through fog
or did it fall through my body
like a stone through air?

Setting My Mother's Hair as an Ars Poetica

First the rollers like a sack of elvers,
elastics in a tangle, the little cups that sit
in one end to stretch everything taut
missing, more often than not, so pins
are called for that will have to be
inveigled into place.

Then the steel comb with the long handle
pointed at the end, good for teasing out
hair to be wound from its tip around
a bristled plastic cone and pinned until
her whole head is armadilloed so tight
she could do a handstand, nothing would shift.

But she won't be doing handstands, not today.

She'll sit under hair that's like corn on the cob,
do the Simplex, smoke Silk Cuts, drink cups of tea
I ferry to her and bide her time for the time it takes
for the hair to set; for the grand unfurl; for

my hands to drain, for the pins and rollers,
comb and all to be lost or landfill,
nothing I've need of, my hair
too short to be set by anyone,
least of all by me.

Imagine the Atlantic as a Journalist

who knows one woman's story
told exactly the right way
could change everything

just as one leaf-full of water
added or removed
makes for a different sea

but what to do then with the leaf:
flatten it, smooth out its small scoop
and set it to float on water

maybe so clear and shallow
it drags a shadow-leaf
across the floor?

for Tommy

Imagine the Atlantic as a Chambermaid

taking from her trolley sheets
yet to be slept on by strangers
and, back braced, four-square
to the base of the bed, wrists
cocked, one corner in each fist,
flicking open the first which,
like a breaker spotted out to sea
pulling on the thread of itself,
sprays whiteness over all the room
before collapsing on a mattress
firm as packed sand, there to be
tucked in, folded and smoothed
so no ripple will ever vex this bed.

The Low Road

Another day this road would be a road
and I'd not be stalled in my little car
being lapped at by a sullen flood
unsure if I should reverse or plough through,
my head a full moon of ice-white fright
this January night a-bloat with darkness
on a low road slumped in overspill
from a lake without a name.

Here's my opt-out. Here's how
I write myself clear,

my headlights puckering the surface
so the black satin of its evening wrap
is something I could draw around me
for a disappearing trick.

Proposition

If I decide to live today as a scarecrow
on the tilled field of my life
           (as if!)
           such that wind chatters me,
rain derides, and traffic on the byroad
tilts my way
           still I am nothing but words on sticks,
liable, both, at so much as
                     crow-squawk
           to up and away   out of this.

Still Life in Marble

Staglieno Cemetery, Genoa, Italy

1

The day is hot. So far this morning
his hand has held true, not a stipple,
not a glitch unwarranted. Some days
his right hand contradicts what his left
(his holding, placid, steadfast left) requires.
He works in shade. A man of means has died
and the dying must be marked in marble
carved to trap not grief but its dramatized affect:
a mantilla so fine it weeps its lace; a boot so certain
it folds the fact of death in every crease.

2

He thinks of his wife walking back this evening
from her mother's house, her hair in a coil
at the neck of her blue dress. He thinks of his son,
all but over that rasp of cough; his daughter,
tilting her chin up when she sings. Rabbit for dinner
and a peach for afterwards. He will eat, say his prayers,
dream of god knows what and tomorrow, come early,
as usual, to pick up where he leaves off now,
his mallet and five chisels wrapped in linen,
laid in the wooden box with his name on it.

3

A mother lifts a child to kiss her grandfather's lips.
Heavy that child for so high a grandfather

and there, yes, the mother's arms are strained,
you can see the flex of them under her dress
and the child who kisses, not quite, those lips
will squirm, you know it, the second afterwards
and demand to be released to no stone kiss,
to the garden where girls play (his daughter too).
But he is not the afterwards. His is now.

4

Yesterday he had dust in his eye
that he scratched, not meaning to;
today he has a stye he imagines bigger
than his head, the way it throbs.

So he carves a pimple in the corner of one eye
of the woman so dedicated to her dutiful grief
she will forever lift her daughter to a kiss
that can neither be taken nor given,
his hand coming between.

A very little pimple only, barely visible,
but his mark, still, the way he might carve
a foot to be his wife's and she to know it
when she sees it, and to peel his peach for him
that evening with her hair loose around her face
the way he loves it, just for him,
smelling of almonds and oranges
as stone never does.

5

The peach, he thinks, will be ripe and sweet,
the skin rhyming with the curve of the face
he carved today which he knows (as he does)
will be what visitors will want to touch
so it stays pure white from rubbing
when the rest is smut-clogged grey.
For luck or for prayer. His hand is the first,
on a child so plausible he almost whispers
he's sorry to be leaving her there.

Tonight he will ask his daughter to sing,
praise the song, no matter what.
Tomorrow he'll unpack his tools, start in again
on poppy seed heads he will carve so fine
you can almost count the seeds inside,
feel them prickle when the wind is up,
so little do they know about stone,
its only future, a snag of heat
turned in to a depth of cold.

6

And this is how we live,
by the power of bodies apt to do
whatever we ask of them
to make us real.

From what I see there is no stye,
nor can my finger feel it out,
this same finger typing words
you could run your own hand over

and feel nothing
or not much

unless it's a sore eye
you lift your hand to,
unless it is dust in your mouth.

Tipping Point

Put your coin in the slot with one clever hand; use the other to angle the chute so the coin falls nicely behind a good clump of coins and when the batten sweeps forward to nudge them all on, a few will cascade over the top ledge to fall nicely behind a good clump of coins and when the batten sweeps forward to nudge them all on a few will cascade over the front ledge to fall out of the game and back into the life you'll just have won.

And if this were a game the batten would not be a solid block of time. The coins would not be years and years and, when you were done, you'd not be running all through the arcade calling out for your father and mother, your dog, only to find yourself in darkness, your hands twiddling emptiness, the coin cold on your tongue.

What the day offers, so the day demands

Sunday morning: bells in a plethora all across town, no two of them leaning into same notes, the air rife with their cut-across and squabble.

Which is as it should be, I should think, this week of all weeks. A monk in the East says we're entering Last Days, but he's young and it's been a good, long while since I believed in monks. That things are perilous is certainly true: war and then another war, and now another in the offing. So many places seem to be either teetering or mired. Despots, with one finger, stir the world.

And still the bells as ever the bells. Earlier the rain was merciless but now the day has rinsed itself clean; is hoist, as they say, onto high ground, from which is visible the town, hunkered down within its commonplace.

Does it comfort me, the sound they make? Does it quell the terror, the outrage? Is it feasible that I, with my tea to drink, my book to read, my poem to write, should decide when I should care?

I woke with bad dreams clogged in my throat so I could hardly breathe.

What will stop when the bells stop, what continue? This much I know: the morning will fill itself in around the slits and stabs of them. I'll breathe in words. This house will stand. The grey sadness of aftermath will hold no sway in the light of afternoon. Even the bad dreams will drain away, at least until when next a day turns inside out and I'm naked to the world, and petrified.

Meanwhile the bells as ever the bells, all of them using the very same voice (as if there were not any others) to say, Still here. Still here.

Still here.

May the Tenth

The way I hear phrases of song jimmying their way
out of rehearsal and into the corner of the street
where I happen to be standing on bars of sunlight
is pretty much how I notice that butterfly's wings
as it chases itself down, very lightly, between stalks
of cow parsley up to my neck, or up into the horse
chestnut's too-churchy candelabra, every blossom
reaching for top C. And it's warm, we all agree

it's warm, and don't we deserve it after all the rain?
A man whistles, a man mows; daisies lean into blades
but oh, the garden chair has never looked so white.
You could call it a perfect day and we do, I do,
twisting light words into papery spills I hope
against hope might yet catch on its fire.

Snapshot

Told, as a child is, to stand over there
(and allowing for this 'there' to be anywhere —
garden, statue, with the old people, the dog —
except, in this case, it is a nook by a bridge
in a town of historical import, it is said)
to be photographed with you as proof
of them having been here, together, once,
on this afternoon and not a duller or even

a brighter one; you in your nylon candy stripes
and your bockety teeth and your standing
half of you scissored in shadow
as your mother, buttoned in silver goats,
and your father, zipped into his voice,
are telling you to smile. And so you do.

Two Kinds of Ending

She'd be waiting; eye to the window,
ear to the door, a day behind her
she thinks of, morning and afternoon,
as two sullen plaits of rain
clipped, tightly, to her skull;

then thinks of him,
feels the silt of him thickening
in her lungs, her throat, her mouth.

If it weren't for the small body
starfished in the top third
of the deep blue bed,
one hand open, the other burled
inside hot milk breath,

she'd tear page 100 from his
every favourite novel, she would;
leave the flitters in the shape of a noose
on the marble countertop.

Let him riddle that in her being gone:
words hard against new edges ripped
by a hand all innocence.

But how can it be?
She asks it, ringless, to budge
the evening a small bit to the right.

There now. Oranges. Plums.

Imagine the Atlantic as a Film-maker

shooting a stop-motion sequence
where an object — surf-board, swimmer, yacht —
shimmies between frames, its every next step
stranded in deep-blue beforethought
or drawn in air so thick with salt
one of it is always ghosting itself
while one of it tries on now for size
and one of it fixes fanciful sights
on an ending out of frame.

Imagine the Atlantic as a Bartender

hands like cormorants skeeting and huzzing
over the polished counter or the taps.

Her job this evening to keep it all smooth
no matter the undertow; to balance
the frisky hen-do in the corner
with the regulars like boulders
on their high stools at the bar.

To take whatever's flung at her,
from banter to jibes to slobber to puke
to coins predictably short.

To know if the laugh breaking over the room
is the kind to flip to blubbing in the loo
come closing time.

To deal out the lines in her head
like a poker flush of small cards only
or waves in the cove where there's never
enough wind to cause a stir,

saying only as much as needs to be said
but making it sound like the first time
every time.

The Future of the Poem

Make a tiny boat of it,
sail it, as John Taylor did,
down the Thames.

        Write your name at the bottom of it.
        Now we're collaborating.

Leave it out on the windowsill
to sweet-talk the rain.

        Hang it from a mulberry bush,
        wait for the wind to read it
        first one way and then another.

        Watch it become something smaller.
        Watch it rot.

See it grow a ruff of fungus
prettier, far, than these words
thought to be.

        Imagine it a page in a book
        rubbing up against other pages.

Then imagine that book
without this page.
Would you call it a loss?

        Wear it close against your skin
        as if it were, again, a shirt.
        A camisole. Chemise.

                Rub it briskly on your wrists
                so it smells as you do.

        Strip it. As in, make strips of it.
        (What did you think I meant?)

Place a flake of it on your tongue
to check for salt or spice.
Also for sweet.

        Block out every second *o*
        call it a partial eclipse.

Trace over the letters in pencil,
then erase. Will the rubbings,
do you think, recall the poem?

                Scrape the letters off the page,
                upcycle to new words.

Draw over it in coloured inks.
Then it can be art.

        Cut into it stick man, stick woman.
        Hang it in your room
        for company.

                Cut into it another word.
                See how white space, its silences,
                persist?

Let that other word be 'love',
the whole poem strained
through the mould of the *o*
at the very heart of it.

        Swap the cut letters,
        shimmy them round;
        try to make them different
        differently.

                Read it aloud so my words
                    infiltrate
                your breath. We're close.

        Leave it alone, why don't you?
        It knows what it's about.

Burn it. But be careful
that you don't burn more than it.

In the Cemetery of Non-existent Cemeteries, Gdańsk

First time, I listened for an hour to the sea bring down
its cudgels on a sullen afternoon. Except I can't have done,
the sea not being within earshot and being a diffident sea.

Second, a glass cube of an hour slipped through my fingers
to smash at my feet. By which time I found the prospect
of a page without a flaw in it unbearable. Third, the pockets

of my houndstooth greatcoat swarming, I went to shake out
perfect ice and pin-tucked sleet over a hole that wasn't there.
If it was a hole. If it was not an altar, the inverse of a grave,

a black granite hole in a view of a park that could look like
a redacted poem on a page, depending on where you stand.
Either way, as I'm guessing you'll have guessed by now

I never visited but the name, which is to say I visit only
the name, if only to think for a moment, even, that here
is somewhere I could live with being forever dead

if I have to be. Which is impossible, of course, for
who could be forever dead in a puzzle that predicts
its solving, under a name with a hyphen in its midst

that might, if pressed correctly, open out into a hinge?

Hindsight

for my brother, Ray

This pipe of light I pull myself through
like a rag through the barrel of a shotgun
to clean it as my father taught me,
unloaded, double-checked, farm gun
spatchcocked on our kitchen table
for the washed-out squares of old
cotton towels and my baby clothes
threaded on a straightened hanger
to be fed in one end and budged all
the way up until out at the muzzle,
two times each barrel, processional,
the rags well-chastened by smut
and grease before I'd flick it,
the shotgun, shut again with a sound
I'd think was like a shot, and lift it,
the shotgun, two hands for the heft,
to carry it over to the tall press
left of the washing machine
and slot it, the shotgun, back between
ironing board and sweeping brush
until the next sign of foxes
in the lambing field but I'd
never see any of that . . .

This pipe of light I pull myself through
is nothing like that one, I suppose,
though my eye is level with its breach
so I can see the last of evening
creep away from the back door.

Short Poem About Self-consciousness

I swim in poems
but breathlessly

and think of myself
when I think of myself
as sheep's wool on barbed wire.

I climb into strangeness
as I climb into madrigals
through tears in the brocade.

Elsewise, I'm showing up at your door
with a face on me, one arm
as long as the other,

everyone inside
clinking their lines,
facing my way
and measuring

with their eyes

but measuring.

Introduction

This poem is about a 1951 Western Union telegram I bought recently in a Cambridge charity shop. Sent from Montreal and addressed to Isaiah Berlin at Lowell House, Harvard University, the telegram reads: 'RING ME IF POSSIBLE ABOUT 9.30 THURSDAY MORNING OR EARLIER LOVE = ELIZABETH ='.

The telegram is, I suspect, from Aline Elisabeth Yvonne Halban, who, five years later, became Berlin's wife. She was then living in Montreal, married to the nuclear physicist, Hans Halban, hence, I think, the slight subterfuge of using her middle name. The misspelling of her name — with a zed rather than an s — is probably an error by the telegrapher.

I'd read this poem for you now, except I can't: it doesn't exist: I haven't written it. I could give it to you in draft form, in the telegraphy code that translates words into semaphore and back at the other end of an electrical connection into legible words, but I find I don't understand that system of applied symbolism.

Plus, the telegram has nothing to do with me and wants nothing to do with me and I admit that, no matter how I try, I'm unable to sweet-talk it into a poem written by me.

The telegram — A5, cellophaned, browned with age — you'll have to visualize for yourselves, just as you'll have to imagine, if you're minded to, the poem.

Imagine the Atlantic as an Artist

stowing a lost gold ring
under layers of ochre, bisque and buff

so you can't see sight nor sign of it
for sand.

She rinses her brushes, washes her hands,
rubs a finger where a ring could be,

thinks how she made gold out of nothing,
then made gold disappear.

for Eve

Imagine the Atlantic as a Poet

finding in the scribble of boats on a deep blue page
lines that could just as well be letters,
letters that could just as well be a word,
a word that could just as well be a promise
windblown as spindrift.

The Copybook

We learned to write in Aisling copybooks,
salmon pink or mossy green, with either a fountain pen
on the front cover, or a round tower over which
a single swallow was caught in the act of circling or alighting,
who could tell, perched in its green sky, in its black outline,
above the tower, which was also black, and gave no hint
of the stowed gold or frightened monks inside.

One was ruled, the other not. One was for Irish,
English, History and Geography; the other, sums,
though that's where I put the poems, of course,
small poems with red titles in the taut blue grid,
like a page of slit windows, crossed with iron bars.

Ending Without a Poem

Why rust patches on the evening sky?
It's not as if I didn't use the day.

My Own Fourth Wall

If I pretend no one's looking at me
or pretend someone is
       and you pretend you're not looking at me
       or you are,

we won't confuse the game of 'poem'
we're playing here,
       will we?

If I prove elusive, so too you,
       (my conjured, deft, obliging you)
both of us sitting in dapple or daub,
       me, dead still with my eyes closed
       eyelids sifting shadow from shade
as a wall does, or a pool;

you, legs dangling, eyes to the line
that separates where we are now
from where we will not be
together
       or nearly,

one of us thinking *company*;
the other, *no you don't*.

But I know if I needed help you'd bring
       the cures of the world
in a grey knapsack hoisted
on your back through a downpour

and were I able to touch your face
with a word of thanks,
well then I'd touch your face,
       you can believe it.

And if either of us knew how to comfort
    the other
then that's what we'd do,
    certainly.

Dive in, says one of us, who cares who,
and something occurs on foot of the saying
    so the page, this page,
    is speckled with affect.

For a second, my hand holds what you hold,
and I swear, hand on heart (for what it's worth)
    if I were able to nudge
    the cold stone of the poem
    past the lip of its stone-cold certainties

    I would. Wouldn't I?

Reading Chinese Love Poems in a Borrowed English House

And we'll dissolve the sorrows of a hundred centuries.
        — from 'Bring in the Wine' by Li Bai (701-761),
        translated by Vikram Seth

A house with centuries stacked inside
like boxes of flat-packed furniture
taking up half the place.

∽

A bed to face the morning sun.
One net curtain
pulses, fills
like music.
Or like news.

∽

Always a crocheted white coverlet
meaning to rhyme with a clean day.

∽

From behind cloud
day blooms in the window;
white chrysanthemum.

∽

Off and on goes traffic
behind the house.
Off and on go voices
carried on a whim.

∽

A morning like four white windowpanes,
its hours all the same size as each other.

∽

When I started
I wrote this house without you.
Then I wrote you in.

∽

Not even the vase of red tulips
is louder than your name.

∽

I place my mouth
to a slit of hope.
I blow.

∽

My damp hand
on a wall:
a kind of print
a day makes
nothing
of.

∽

A Tallis motet
and I am back
to this house
being built
course by course
up to the
coping stone.

Mid-morning folds itself across
like a sheet of A4
with words meaning
to hide.

The Dutch Gable
kindly straddles
all accents, even mine,
wishing to think themselves
home.

Courtyard pebbles lodged
in my shoes
score the kitchen lino: Jazz.

East is centuries, one by one;
west is a main road.
Here is a page of sunlight
with your name written on.

∽

The courtyard is a pocket mirror
the day keeps checking
for lines.

∽

The gutters
on the old row houses
slump a little
this low afternoon.

∽

The gardener rakes
the courtyard gravel
in circles
keeping time
with the oak tree.

∽

A river once flowed
in front of the house:
it might have brought
casks of grain and wine
and spools of thread
and you.

∽

Once the sun trips over
the gable wall
I will lose sight of this.

∽

It ought to be raining
in your absence;
it ought to be thunder
and snow.

∽

Fruit from the arbutus
squished in my sole
has a tale for the kitchen floor
of hills and moons,
of faraway, of dew.

∽

If I sing this afternoon
it is only for the chairs and table,
only for the room.

∽

Church bells, faintly.
I grow old
in the silence
either side.

∽

The day sits down
on the low stone wall
between the oak
and all the rest.

Antique dusk
with its yellowing pages
as of yet uncut.

So, why do I leave my curtains parted
though it is late
and the gate has been locked?
No one comes this way.

And still the oak tree
down in the courtyard
holds itself still
as if candles are lit
at the tip of every branch.

The courtyard's deserted
but for a full moon
pencilling in
slates and rooflines;
but for me, watching it.

Moonlight pooled in the courtyard;
that's how you kiss my hand.

Through tonight's black window, stars.
This too is a poem with you in it.

∽

The bedroom window
I leave on the latch
for the night to step in
in its soft-soled shoes
to wake no one but me.

∽

I read Li Bai;
the same moon
give or take
the self-same solitude.
I too fill a cup of wine
raise it with the hand
that writes these words,
to a mouth that is speaking yours.

∽

Somewhere — a drain
or a sewer, perhaps,
or in the fold
behind a rhyme —
a DNA fleck knowing
what I know
bides its time.

∽

So, you, half a world yonder:
are you lodged already
in my clean tomorrow
or lost to me in mine own
been-and-gone?

∽

Four centuries under me
in the bed
creak when I turn over,
sag when I dream
and speckle my dust,
as if I too
were riddled
with time.

Acknowledgements

page 41 In the early 1600s, John Taylor (known as The Water Poet) sailed, for a bet, in a boat made of brown paper, down the Thames. Although the venture failed, Taylor nonetheless recorded it in his poem 'The Praise of Hempseed', published in 1620, noting:
'The water to the Paper being got,
In one halfe houre our boat began to rot:
The Thames (most lib'rall) fild her to the halves,
Whilst Hodge and I sate liquoured to the calves.'

Acknowledgements are due to the editors of the following publications where some of these poems, or versions of them, were published first:
'*Mise en Scène*' and 'Proposition', *Archipelago*
'Still Life in Marble', *Hudson Review*
'Imagine the Atlantic as an Actor', *New York Review of Books*
'Two Kinds of Ending', *The New Yorker*
'Lint', *Poetry Ireland Review*
'Hindsight', *Poetry London*
'Infinity Pool', *Poetry Magazine*
'Inner Space', *The Poetry Review*
'Stansted to Knock, December 21st', *Times Literary Supplement*
'Tipping Point' and '*An Poll Gorm* / The Blue Pool', *Winter Papers*

'The Copybook' was included in *Eamon at 80*, a Festschrift for Eamon Grennan published by The Gallery Press in 2022.

I'm grateful to Conor O'Callaghan for his eagle-eyed reading of this book in manuscript. Thanks too to Peter Fallon and the team at The Gallery Press for all their generous help with this book, and for all they do.